contents

preface

This booklet has been produced in response to requests from Guiders and Commissioners following the first Reach Out and Recruit campaign in 2000.

Many units, Districts, Divisions and Counties held events during the autumn of 2000. Some successfully recruited new adults to join them. Others gained publicity or more interest from girls but didn't gain as many adults as they would have liked.

From the follow-up research, it appeared that often what people were looking for was a bit more help in the whole process of recruiting adults. What else was needed? What happened after you had handed out your postcards? How do you turn an event into a recruitment and PR initiative?

The purpose of this booklet is to give a number of special event activities that can be run in units, Districts, Divisions and then show how they can be used for recruitment and PR.

The booklet is in three parts: the Introduction with Principles of PR and Recruitment; the Fun Events and the Appendices (containing Template Press Releases, a sample Questionnaire, and other materials). We hope you will find it helpful. Let us know how you get on by returning the Evaluation Form at the back of the book.

We wish you success with your recruitment.

Pauline McKie, Working Group Chairperson 2001

BROWNIES

introduction

Why a Fun Events Booklet for Recruitment?

Simple really. The best way to recruit is to ask someone directly. Nothing beats the face to face approach but, having said this, many of us would find it difficult to go up to someone and say, 'You'd make a really good Brownie Guider'. In fact, a lot of us would probably find it difficult to strike up conversation with anyone who isn't part of our daily lives.

The fun event acts as a 'hook' to give you a common topic of conversation with people you may not know that well. This then opens up the possibility of a genuine exchange of information and a chance to learn something about other people.

A good example of this method of recruitment was at the STOMP day to celebrate the year 2000. One County arranged a day out at a theme park for every member. Of course, the Rainbows and Brownies needed extra adults to accompany them so their mums came to the rescue. For one Division group it became a recruitment opportunity they hadn't anticipated. The mums' discovered that the leadership team were friendly people who enjoyed being together with the girls. The girls were pleased to welcome new adults to the group, were co-operative and generally helpful. After all, few people would wish to give up their free time to a group that doesn't have some of these qualities. So, when the Guiders were discussing the possibility of opening a new Brownie Pack in the area and recruiting more leaders, it was great when a mum unexpectedly said, 'Which night are you thinking of running it?'. The Division team didn't need a second hint and immediately followed up this opportunity.

More often than not, these unexpected opportunities for recruitment arise from a planned event or occasion. This booklet contains a number of suggestions for fun events involving parents and friends, but no doubt you will have lots of your own ideas. If so, please share them with us by sending it to the Membership Development Manager (at CHQ in London) and also feel free to adapt any activity to suit your needs and objectives.

Enjoy your fun event and remember, if you get one or two offers of help, not necessarily as adult leaders, you've done well but make sure you follow up those offers as soon as you can. Once you've recruited new helpers, why not involve the new recruits in the next planned fun event? For instance, if you manage to attract people from the Celebrating Mothering Sunday event, you could suggest they participate in the Family Fun Day, or the Family Trail. This would provide an exciting initiation into Guiding, and a good continuity to your recruitment campaign.

Principles of PR and Recruitment

PR

The events listed in this booklet vary considerably. There will be some events of more interest to your local media than others. However, it is always worth bearing in mind that if your event is fun, involves members of your local community and provides a good photo opportunity, your local press may well be interested.

Photography is a good way to advertise Guiding in your local community. However, please be aware that if the photography is of a member under 16, you will need to obtain parental permission before the picture is used. The G/O form for information and consent on a one day activity is the usual method of gaining permission and you must highlight that the photographs can be used for future publicity.

If you are not sure of the best route to take regarding publicity and local coverage, contact your District, Division or County, PR Adviser or even your local paper directly, and ask them what they would cover, they may be able to guide you in the right direction. Ultimately, remember that local media want to cover new and exciting events in their local area, so try to give them something different to report about!

Recruitment

Before you run any activity with recruitment as either the main purpose or a welcome offshoot, you need to think about how you are going to deal with recruitment issues. Do you know what help you need and where? Think about how flexible you can be if someone offers to help but it cannot be a regular, weekly commitment. You can't afford to turn down that offer but how can you make good use of it? What about job share, could it work in your unit or area? Think about the value of involving someone for an occasional task and then at a later stage they may wish to become more involved in the organisation.

The Guide Association Recruitment Toolkit helps you think about these issues and plan your recruitment strategy. Why not talk to someone who's been on a Toolkit training and have a look at the Toolkit for yourself or better still ask for your own District, Division or County Toolkit training and get your own copy.

With the best will in the world some people can still find it difficult to approach others with a view to recruiting them into the organisation. That's not a problem. Everyone should be encouraged to be their normal friendly selves and not worry about recruitment just think about giving a positive image of Guiding. However, there will be at least one person you know who has the knack of being able to chat to anyone, is very enthusiastic about Guiding, is interested in other people and smiles a lot. The smile is particularly important. So if you can't be a sales person for the Association, then find someone in your District or County who can and involve them in your plans and ideas for recruitment.

Each of these events can be used for recruitment but remember they are about fun first. Don't get carried away with the hard sell, people will feel threatened, not invited. As part of this approach, refreshments have never been so important, it is often at the time when people are having a drink or food that they're at their most relaxed and sociable. This is the time to recruit. Remember everyone can be a recruiter, from Rainbows to Trefoil Guild. Don't dismiss the power of a Brownie Six asking an adult to be a helper or a leader.

notes

- ***Please remember that a G/O form of consent must be sent out to all parents if you are taking the girl(s) on a one day activity where they will not be present. The G/O form must be completed if photos of an under 16-year old will be taken and published.***
- ***Throughout this publication the word 'parent' or 'mother' has been used for simplicity, but this refers to any legal guardian of the child.***

quiz night

Aim
An evening with parents, friends and older children, who team up for a quiz. Principally, this is a fundraising event with an entry fee for the quiz and raffles.

What you need
- ★ posters and leaflets to advertise the event
- ★ Quizmaster with lots of ready prepared questions
- ★ small speaker system with microphone
- ★ raffle tickets
- ★ prizes including the 'booby' prize
- ★ tables and chairs
- ★ pencils and paper
- ★ Guide displays around the room
- ★ a jolly atmosphere

Outline of what to do
The Quizmaster asks the questions and teams of about four or six people have to answer correctly to score points. During the interval a raffle takes place and refreshements may be served. Prizes are awarded for first, second, third and, of course, the 'booby'.

Size of event
As many as there is room for in the chosen venue.

Time
Notification
One month before the night.
Preparation
Long enough to advertise the quiz night effectively and book a Quizmaster (for a small fee) or you could prepare your own questions. Attend one or two pub quizzes and you'll soon get the idea and there are lots of books of quiz questions in the shops now. A team of two or three people could soon put this event together with the minimum of effort.

Venue
The traditional venue is a social club or pub where there is a bar available, but this may make it difficult for young people to attend. The community or village hall or Guide hut will do fine and if alcohol is acceptable in the venue then people can bring their own refreshments.

Age
All ages would enjoy this, but make sure the teams are mixed, and there are questions for all years (children who are very young might not be so interested).

Guest list
Ask the President, Commissioner or another appointment holder if she and her family would like to take part and present the prizes at the end.

Which season?
An evening at any time of the year, if you arrange it in winter make sure the venue is warm.

Costs involved
- ★ printing of leaflets and posters to advertise the event
- ★ prizes
- ★ raffle tickets
- ★ refreshments
- ★ fee for Quizmaster

It is normal to charge a small entry fee of about £2.00 per head and then for raffle tickets. Various local businesses or friends of Guiding may donate the raffle prizes.

What to wear
Definitely casual.

PR opportunities available
Approach local businesses to see if they are able to donate prizes.

Recruitment opportunities to consider
Make sure that Guiders who enjoy chatting to people get around as many groups as possible in the interval. The chat doesn't have to be about recruitment, just thank people for coming. Perhaps think about putting in the quiz a few questions on Guiding, with modern aspects as well as a few historical ones. Most of the questions are verbally asked, but in some cases a hand-out is given (eg. with pictures of pop-stars to be named). On these sheets (or on a separate piece of paper, one for each table) you could print at the bottom some lines like, 'Can you help backstage at the Gang Show?', 'We need help with <x, y, z> are you free?', 'It's a Knockout takes place on <date>, players needed!', 'Be an Ambassador for Guiding'.

If you have an Ambassador who is willing to come to the event, a Guiding person could introduce them at the beginning of the second half, when everyone has relaxed. The Ambassador could say a few words about what they do as an Ambassador and ask others to volunteer (in this capacity or in any other way). At the end of the quiz, Guiders can remind people of the different types of help that are needed and make themselves available should anyone want to talk to them.

celebrating
mothering
sunday

Aim

To plan an event where members can entertain mothers with a sit-down meal, prepared and served by the girls. This activity will enable the unit team to give people outside of Guiding a snapshot view of the Movement at its best. The girls will have the opportunity to show their entertaining skills so they can demonstrate the programme whilst promoting Guiding at the same time.

What you need

A team of people to assist the girls, you may wish to bring in outside experts to achieve the best possible results but it should be a fun experience for the girls too, not a daunting one. You'll also need:

- ★ craft materials
- ★ table cloths
- ★ cutlery
- ★ crockery
- ★ trays
- ★ a reasonably well stocked kitchen
- ★ some music

Outline of what to do

At the beginning, have a brainstorm to get ideas from the girls, or speak to someone in catering. During the weeks before, prepare everything you will need. This will allow the young people to make choices and have a real input, particularly in helping choose the menu. Remember to consider vegetarians and special dietary requirements, making sure there are choices for everyone.

Before the event, divide the girls into groups and organise who will do what. Girls who enjoy crafts can be in charge of making invitations, place names, napkin folding , menus, flowers for the table. Hostesses can be responsible for laying the table, serving the food and planning what is on the menu. Cooks can arrange a session where they make simple dishes (some of which can be made and frozen ready for the day). Or you might do the preparation over several weeks so that all the girls can do a bit of each element.

Size of event

One guest per girl.

Time

Notification

One month.

Preparation

Four weeks.

Venue

Large meeting hall with a kitchen, table and chairs.

Age

Most effective with the Brownie section but could be adapted for all sections making it easier for Rainbows and more challenging for Guides and Senior Section.

Guest list

Mother for each girl. District Commissioner or someone not involved in the unit who could be a 'floater', ie. able to chat to mums while in-between courses.

Which season?

Spring, for Mothering Sunday.

Costs involved

The unit will need some funds to purchase in advance the food and craft materials. After dinner you might want to pass round the chefs' hats for any donations.

What to wear

Guides or Brownies can wear their uniform with aprons, some in chefs' hats. Mums could be asked to dress more formally.

PR opportunities available

- ★ Send out post-event press release (see Appendices, page 23)
- ★ Take photographs of event and distribute with release.
- ★ Contact a local college for help with catering or other activities, or even arrange a visit to a catering college or large hotel for the girls to see how big kitchens work.

Recruitment opportunities to consider

The target group will be the guests so an open invitation could be distributed to guests to help with the next project. The success of the event will act as a powerful recruitment tool. Decide what you are going to do next so that you can include this in your message on the night. Remember, enjoyment on the night breeds successful recruiting, people want to be part of something good. In your message, as well as thanking the girls, tell them a little about how not only the girls have benefitted but the adults have learnt too – you'll usually be able to find a few things. Look out for the mum who might speak on behalf of the others to thank the girls and leaders. She might be worth following up.

fashion

Aim
An opportunity to encourage Guides and Brownies to think creatively, work as a team, and actively show the fun and friendliness of Guiding to people. It's an event that could be used as a fundraiser too.

What you need
- ★ old clothes, either from a charity shop, jumble sale, or at the back of Auntie Hilda's wardrobe! Clothes can also be recycled and reinvented from jumble or bin-liners, be creative and let the girls really run wild with their imagination
- ★ make-up (if you are feeling daring)
- ★ small speaker system with microphone
- ★ chairs for guests
- ★ music and decoration

Outline of what to do
Decide on a theme for the fashion show eg. Bad Taste, The Sixties, the Jumble Ball, Space Walk. Once the girls have selected their clothes, get them into their Sixes or Patrols and ask them to write a short piece describing what they are wearing which can be used as a narrative during the show itself. Something along the lines of: 'Next we have Sarah. Sarah is sporting a lime green 60s style jacket with red trim. Her long flowing red skirt was the height of fashion in the 80s, and is complimented by her red and black stilettos, which once belonged to her mother. Sarah has chosen a lime green clutch bag, and black hair bow as her finishing touches.'

Each girl can take it in turns or nominate just one person to do the announcing, but let them have a practice run before their parents arrive. You could play some music as the girls are strutting down the catwalk.

As a finale, have all the girls come back onto the catwalk for a final twirl.

Size of event
This is a unit or District event, to which parents and other guests might be invited.

Time
Notification
At least a month before the show.

Preparation
The Guides and Brownies are encouraged to obtain their own items of clothing but organisation of the show will need some preparation and rehearsal. A few weeks should be enough for this but it will depend on the scale of event you're undertaking.

Venue
Hall large enough for the girls to walk up and down with chairs either side, giving the appearance of a catwalk. Toilets or another room for the girls to get changed in and preferably a room for the girls to wait in before making their big entrance.

Age
Brownies or Guides.

Guest list
Parents, other family members, local Guiders and units, Ambassadors and other people in your community.

Which season?
Any time of year. It is a good idea to tag this onto a fundraising event like a jumble sale or car boot sale, which allows the girls to get their costumes out of what is remaining and might otherwise be thrown away. Costumes could be sold on afterwards to help with funding.

Costs involved
A few pence at the most, but this activity need not cost you anything, just a little imagination. You could consider the event as a fundraiser and charge a small admittance.

What to wear
Guiders should be in uniform.

PR opportunities available
- ★ To maximise number of visitors, hold in conjunction with another event, ie. a local fashion show, fête, roadshow, community show.
- ★ Take photos of event and distribute to press with a press release afterwards.

Recruitment opportunities to consider
If you or the girls make a programme for the event you could highlight some future activities and the help you need. At a suitable time in the evening (perhaps the end) a member (or leader) can stand up and say a few words. They can refer to the 'help wanted' list and encourage people to get involved. Remember, girls can be powerful advocates.

reception for ambassadors

Aim
An evening buffet party to raise County profile and to give an opportunity for newly appointed Ambassadors to meet members of the Association in all sections, to hear of the achievements and pass on the message!

What you need
Food and drink and helpers. If you've built the evening into your budget it is worth having caterers! The real advantage of having wine and fruit juice and mixed canapés served by professional staff is that as the food is brought around on trays, it allows everyone to form natural small groups without Guiders worrying too much about looking after the guests.

Outline of what to do
Write to units, Districts and Divisions asking for suggestions of people who could be Ambassadors. Selecting people with a high local profile is always an advantage, eg. local celebrities, local TV personalities, mayors, councillors; people in community jobs and local education, ie. headteachers, caretakers and coach organisers! And anybody else who helps and supports the Association. Send a letter to as many people as possible, if you don't ask, you won't get! At the same time as inviting them to be an Ambassador, ask if they are able to attend the special reception (see Appendices, page 18 for a sample invitation letter).

At the event, have a limited number of short speeches. For instance, the County Commissioner might say a welcome; a Young Leader or Ranger could say a few words about Guiding from their point of view, especially if they've had international experience; and another Senior Section member could endorse the role of Ambassadors, saying what they have signed up to do and how they can help the Association.

Size of event
Aim to invite and cater for roughly 20 to 30 Ambassadors. Aim to have approximately two members for every guest, depending on the total capacity of the venue.

Time
Notification
Write letters to Guiders in your County for suggestions about four months before the date of the evening. Then letters of invitation to the Ambassadors about three months before the night (if you expect fewer responses, then two months should be enough).

Preparation
It is important that the Guiders and the girls understand that their role for the evening is to be positive and promote Guiding. Issue a briefing sheet to all the County representatives beforehand and also hold a short meeting before the guests arrive. The most important instruction should be: 'circulate, smile and mix with the guests!'.

Set up a professional looking display using boards and materials from Reach Out and Recruit and/or the banners from CHQ to provide a focal point in the room for photographs and presentation of badges. Include in the display some good quality photographs of local Guiding (enlarged and laminated will make them look very impressive).

Invite members of the County to attend as welcoming and enthusiastic hosts to sell the image of Guiding as being exciting and vibrant. Senior Section girls can welcome guests on arrival. All members and guests should be wearing a badge for easy recognition throughout the evening.

Venue
Hire an appropriate sized hall. A venue with good cloakroom facilities to accomodate all the guests' coats and outdoor wear, and catering facilities – or at least a room for preparation and storage.

Age
Have a good mix of members there, young Guiders, Senior Section members and Guides and if some units can bring a few Brownies and Rainbows that would be a very balanced representation. Be careful that the ratios do not exceed three to one as regards members to guests.

Guest list
Newly appointed Ambassadors and County members.

Which season?
Any time is a good time for this kind of reception.

Costs involved
- ★ sending out all invitation letters and follow-up
- ★ hire of the venue and for the caterers
- ★ purchase of Ambassador cards and badges

What to wear
Guiders and girls to be in smart uniform.

PR opportunities available
Take photos during the evening and send to the local press. Keep them for future publicity. Have an Ambassador photographed formally (ie. with the County Commissioner and girls). You may decide to send the Ambassador a copy afterwards.

Recruitment opportunities to consider
When you are planning your reception, think of who in the community you would like to attend. People such as local youth workers, council officials, MPs, councillors and business leaders are excellent people to invite to help spread the word about Guiding. You may also want to invite local celebrities, your Mayor, and any one else that has a high profile within your area.

Ambassadors don't have to be people previously involved in or supportive of Guiding. You should use this opportunity to reach new people. Once appointed as an Ambassador, these people will help your recruitment campaign by speaking to their peers and colleagues about The Guide Association and increasing awareness in your community.

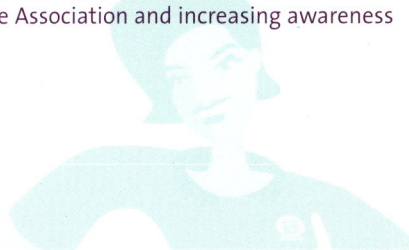

visit

to the zoo

Aim

An organised trip to the local zoo providing a great day out for children and their parents which emphasises the educational and enjoyment value of Guiding. This could be a chance to use 'the Guiding Bug' that has formed a part of Reach Out and Recruit 2001. There might be a creative activity using the 'bug' you can plan to do in the zoo, or the possibility to find out about real bugs.

What you need

- ★ information on the entrance fee to the zoo (most zoos offer a group discount)
- ★ details of the cost of transport to and from the zoo
- ★ a group organiser pack (usually available from the zoo's educational department) which will contain a map, information on the animals, routes around the zoo, health and safety information, details about catering facilities, toilets and aids for people with disabilities
- ★ the opportunity to meet the bugs 'face to face'
- ★ a letter to parents outlining date, time, place, cost, what to bring, or a G/O form if their child is coming without them
- ★ Guiding Bugs (optional)

Outline of what to do

Some children will be with their parents but others on their own so there must be enough adults to help with their supervision. Try to visit the zoo beforehand, from the point of view of being a group leader this would be a good idea so that you have knowledge about where to find toilets, gift shop etc. Then make a plan with things to do and see which includes free time to wander around. The plan could include a zoo quiz (speak to the education department at the zoo for ideas and hand out the quiz at the beginning of the day), meeting up for feeding time at the lions, a picnic lunch (you could buy the ice creams!) and why not ask the zoo if they could put on a special insect display. Often they will bring a Tarantula to stroke or a land snail to hold as well as other things to look at. Remember to check for any phobias or allergies.

Size of event

As many people as you can effectively manage.

Time

Notification

At least two months before the day is planned.

Preparation

6 weeks.

Venue

The local zoo.

Age

All.

Guest list

Friends, family and members of the Association.

Which season?

This event would be better in the summer months, check that the zoo is open before you announce plans.

Costs involved

- ★ letter advertising the event
- ★ payment for coach and entrance fee from childrens' parents

What to wear

Uniforms are useful for finding people and good for promoting our image whilst having a fun day out. If the zoo is a popular venue with Guiding groups then neckers are also helpful for easy identification.

PR opportunities available

Take photos of the day out and distribute afterwards to the local media and to the zoo itself for their internal publication.

Recruitment opportunities to consider

Relax and enjoy the day with the girls and other adults. There's so much to see in the modern zoo that the group could easily drift off in all directions, that's fine but key times might be when everyone meets up for lunch or on the journey home when they've had a good day. Chat about Guiding issues in a positive manner but don't go over the top. On the way home, hand out an Evaluation Form for everyone to fill in with an extra question or two for those parents who came along to help out (see example in Appendices, page 28).

family trail

Aim
A walking trail around the unit's local area including all family members. This kind of game is great for teamwork and co-operation as well as fun outdoors.

What you need
* first aid cover
* co-ordinator
* activity sheets with instructions for trail and pencils
* clock (to time entrants)
* refreshments and someone to prepare and serve them
* person to mark the completed activity sheet at the end
* prizes
* Guiding Bugs (optional)

Outline of what to do
A walking trail is suitable for all the family. Leaders, Young Leaders or Senior Section members could be asked to write the instructions and families of a unit asked to participate. Each family or group are given instructions and when directed, walk along a route as detailed. The instructions should include questions to be answered as the family follows the route. These questions should be varied – simple ones for the younger members and more challenging ones for the older. They may also be asked to collect items on the way. Once the hunt is finished, questions are marked and a note of the time it has taken for the family to complete the route is made. The family with the most correct answers are the winners and if there is a tie-break,the time taken to complete the course is the deciding factor.

Don't forget to advise the police, and neighbours if you will be taking a route around a residential area, and to check for safety.

Size of event
Minimum of two families, but the groups can be mixed with adults and children from different families. This could be run at unit or District level.

Time
Notification
A few months in advance of the trail, send letters to those who might be interested, and follow up letter three weeks before the actual day.

Preparation
This will depend on how long you want your hunt to last. Preparing for the event will probably take several hours. First go and decide on your route. Then retrace the route noting directions and looking for clues ie. turn left as you leave the meeting place; what brand of ice cream do they sell at the shop?; how much does a tube of smarties cost?; how many trees at no. 10?; what is the house next door called?; what should you beware of at no. 16? You can also ask each family to collect items on the way such as a feather or a black stone... But remember to check your direction and clues just before the event. Things often change! If you are making this into a bug event you could position bugs in strategic places and tell people they have so many to find on route. If the trail is being done where there are shops nearby, you could ask if the bugs could be hidden somewhere inside. Remember to ensure they can't be moved or taken by other people.

Venue
This event could be held in a village, town or city as long as it is safe to walk around the trail area. Make sure the start and finish point are big enough for everyone. Have refreshments available at the end (possibly even extend the event with a barbecue) which gives leaders more chance to chat with parents etc.

Age
Suitable for any age group.

Guest list
Families of unit members and perhaps a VIP to present the prizes.

Which season?
Summer.

Costs involved
* prizes for the winners
* photocopying activity sheets
* refreshments

What to wear
Any clothing suitable according to the weather!

PR opportunities available
* Contact your local newspaper, radio or tv station – would they like to make up a team?
* Take pictures of the event to release afterwards.

Recruitment opportunities to consider
Talk to mums, aunts, grandparents – all family members. You never know, they may have had such a good time they would like to come along every week and help! Have some details available of specific tasks and events you need help with in the unit or District.

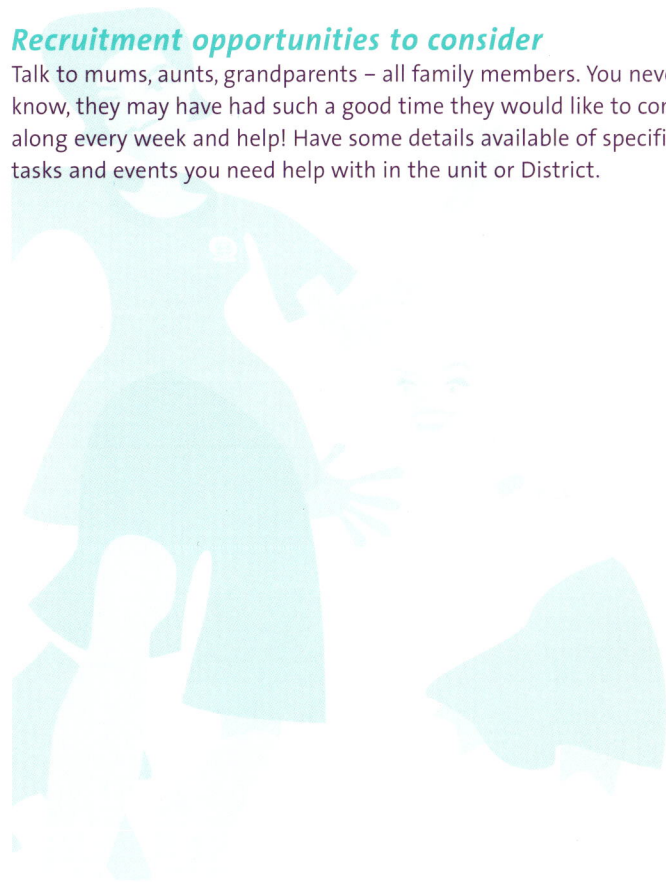

pampering evening

Aim
An evening of pampering and talking about Guiding in this relaxing environment where parents, friends and families can try a range of therapies at little or no cost.

What you need
★ a central booking system (eg. a form in the meeting hall or a telephone number to call)
★ plenty of posters to advertise the event
★ a written agreement should be drawn up to include cost (if the people providing treatments are charging a fee) and indemnity against claim. Check the beauty therapists have a thorough training, or are a member of the appropriate trade organisation
★ people willing to do these activities at no or low cost (try the local college, local health and beauty shops, the gym)
★ a hall big enough to do the activites (or plenty of small rooms) with screens to ensure privacy
★ a good organiser to ensure everybody is where they should be
★ members of the unit to act as hostesses and welcomers, taking people to their appointment
★ a waiting area and something for people to do (or Brownies to entertain them)
★ drinks and snacks for people whilst they are waiting
★ equipment and facilities for the therapists if they do not bring their own

After the event
★ written thanks to those who helped with supplying treatments

Outline of what to do
People book up for their treatment beforehand (and must give 24 hour notice if cancelling), then on the night, they turn up and either pay one price to cover all activities they participate in or pay for each activity they do. The list of treatments could include: massage, aromatherapy, reflexology, face masks, manicures, pedicures, makeovers. Find out how long the treatment will take and book people in regular intervals eg. one person every 30 minutes. Then let them enjoy!

Size of event
The sky's the limit. Work on the basis of one person providing treatments for about eight people so if you have ten activities that's enough for 80 people. If numbers get particulary high for a certain treatment, it might be easier to ask the therapist for group demonstrations. Or, if there is a treatment which is unusual then a group presentation would be a good idea, for example not many people may have heard of reiki healing but might like to!

Time
Notification
Four to six weeks.

Preparation
Quite a bit of pre-event preparation needed but this can be divided up between team members:
★ administration and booking
★ publicity and PR on the night
★ allow plenty of time to find people willing to provide the treatments (although in a small town, people may know others who they can refer you to)

Venue
Hall ideally with plenty of small rooms that can be used, or screens in a large hall. You also need access to water for hot drinks and for use in the treatments.

Age
Depends on the treatment so check with the practitioners if there are any age (or health) limits to the treatment. This may work best when it is open to adults only. Consider having a ladies only night for Mothering Sunday.

Guest list
County/Division/District Commissioner/President and Ambassadors; whoever rents out your premises to you (eg. headteacher, vicar); press; specialist health and beauty magazines etc., parents, mothers and relatives, friends, people from local community groups. If you have a big enough event, do a leaflet for all other organisations that use your venue and any local businesses in the area.

Which season?
An afternoon or evening during the week in the spring or summer when people feel like going out. If you are planning a big event, arrange it for one day over the weekend. If you wanted to get some keen college students to do the treatments for practice and for free (or little cost) then wait until the end of a college term when students have graduated and then fix a date.

Costs involved
Unless the people doing the treatments are prepared to donate use of materials as well as time, you will need to cover all costs in the price of your treatments (make sure you agree these beforehand). Other items to be costed will be hire of hall, drinks, leaflets and posters advertising the event.

What to wear
Guiders who are participating in event could be in uniform so they are easily identified, people coming for treatments can be casual.

PR opportunities available
★ Contact local beauty salons or stores before the event. Do they have any promotions you and your unit can try out?
★ Take photos for your annual report or local paper.

Recruitment opportunities to consider
Probably the best time to try to recruit is when people are waiting for their appointment. The 'soft' sales approach will probably work best, having a display up in the waiting area, asking people to fill in a questionnaire (adapt ideas from the Toolkit), talking to them when showing them to their appointment. If this evening works well, organise another one for a whole day, perhaps calling it a 'Mother and Daughter Day'. This will be another chance to talk to others about Guiding and how people can assist.

it's a knockout

    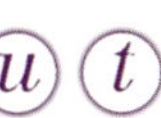

Aim

An afternoon of crazy games and activities in which teams of girls, with parents, compete for the highest score and the prize. During the event there should be opportunities to approach adults for support for Guiding.

What you need

- ★ first aid cover
- ★ suitable venue with large outdoor space
- ★ list of games and activities and the equipment to play them (see Appendices, pages 19–21 for suggested games)
- ★ people to help run the games
- ★ small speaker system for the person in charge and keeping scores
- ★ soft drinks for the participants and refreshments for the spectators
- ★ prizes
- ★ Guiding Bugs (optional)

Outline of what to do

Two or three people should be able to plan the event, book the venue, devise the games, make decisions about the programme of activities, how scoring will take place and so on. On the day, extra help will be required as you will need someone to act as Master of Ceremonies and helpers to assist with the setting up of games, refreshments and parking and act as starters and scorers.

Size of event

This is the ideal event for a group of units in a District or village or urban community where many people know each other and they can relax and have fun together. Six teams of six would be ideal, more than ten teams and it might be difficult to organise, although it has been done before! An afternoon would be a sufficient amount of time.

Time

Notification

A couple of months.

Preparation

About four weeks.

Venue

A place with a large hall for wet weather and an open space for fine weather would be best. Perhaps a school, local campsite or Scout and Guide hut with its own grounds. If the location is especially attractive, encourage family groups to bring a picnic.

Age

All ages can be catered for.

Guest list

Invite local Commissioners to award the prizes.

Which season?

The summer months would be best when you have a good chance of warm weather and no one should mind the occasional dousing with water.

Costs involved

- ★ prizes
- ★ equipment and material for games
- ★ refreshments
- ★ printing of invitations

What to wear

Sports clothes (t-shirts, shorts), things that don't matter if they get wet or covered with foam. It would be helpful if the Guiders wore uniform so that people know who they are. Everyone should be encouraged to bring any special items for games and outdoor wear just in case the weather turns bad.

PR opportunities available

- ★ Distribute a press release outlining the event.
- ★ Contact local tv and radio to see if they would be interested in coming along.
- ★ Get in touch with local businesses to see if they are interested in taking part.
- ★ Contact a local celebrity to see if they would like to open the event – this will attract media interest.
- ★ Take photos of the day and distribute after the event with a press release.

Recruitment opportunities to consider

Make the most of this opportunity to chat to parents. Don't let it get in the way of the games but you could talk to people informally between events or over refreshments. Have a few roles and tasks in mind to ask for help with. Remember, assistance with short-term, one-off tasks might lead to other things.

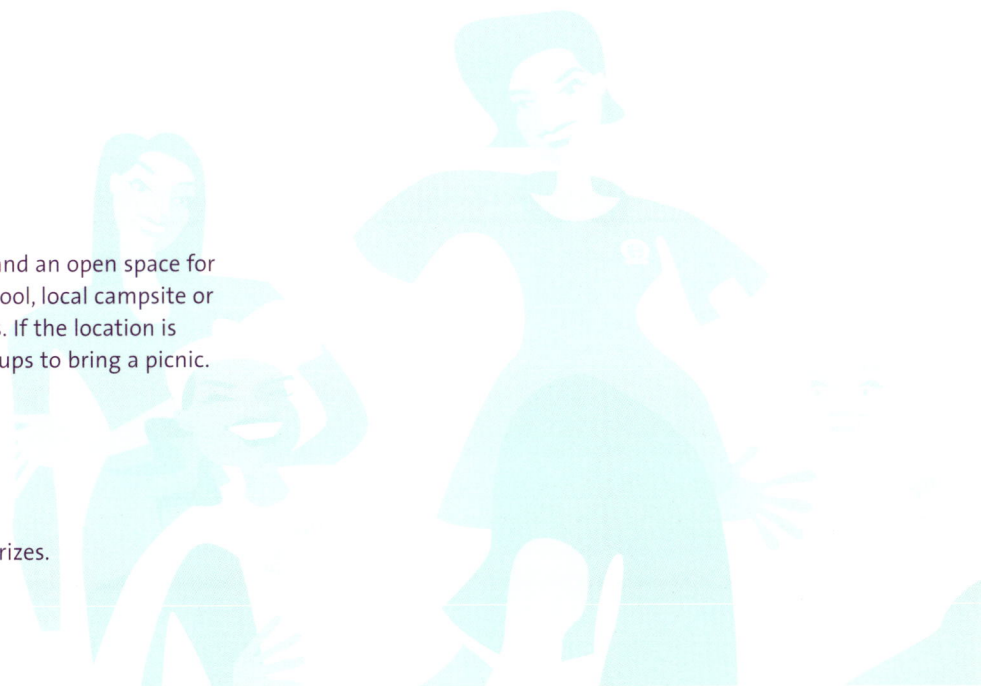

family fun day

Aim
An afternoon or evening of fun for the family including a number of incentives (ie. family challenges and prizes) and a chance to experience first-hand the value of Guiding and enjoyment gained from working with young people. You could include a Guiding Bug activity in one of the games.

What you need
- ★ first aid cover
- ★ a planning team
- ★ ideas and equipment for activities for all ages
- ★ Guiders to run each activity (if this is a District event then each set of Unit Guiders might run one activity)
- ★ Family Fun Day tickets
- ★ a plan for how the activities will be run, ie. a circuit where groups move from one activity to the next available works well
- ★ refreshments and a team to dispense them
- ★ a budget to cover materials, prizes, hire of venue etc.
- ★ Guiding Bugs (optional)

Outline of what to do
For those who haven't run a fun day, here are a few thoughts:
- ★ Girls and adult relatives come along to try their hand at a number of 'just for fun' activities.
- ★ People may come and go, some will stay long enough to complete the family challenge, details of which will be on the tickets. Those who do complete it will be awarded a small token as a prize.
- ★ Tickets will have a lucky number on and should be given to each girl about three weeks before the event. On the day, the lucky number will be cut off the ticket and put in a box to be drawn later. The rest of the ticket is used as a scorecard for the family challenge.
- ★ Refreshments are provided, perhaps served by Rangers and Young Leaders and opportunities are found to chat to people about Guiding and opportunities to help.

Size of event
This will be based on number tickets, size of your venue and how many helpers there are (ie. local Guiders, Unit Helpers and Young Leaders). If you indicate that people may come along during a certain time of day (perhaps on the ticket) then you'll have a decent crowd of people creating a good atmosphere (to avoid some families arriving when no one else is there).

Time
Notification
Two to three months.

Preparation
Although this sounds as though it takes a lot of organising, once the planning team has decided on date, time, venue and the outline programme, you'll only need time for:
- ★ a small planning team to come up with good activity ideas for a wide age range; to deal with administration and finance; to enthuse other Guiders in the locality or District to get involved and to run the activities
- ★ Guiders to prepare for their activity and obtain the equipment and materials
- ★ printing the tickets with all the information
- ★ distributing the tickets to the unit members then allowing about two to three weeks before the event

Unit Guiders can promote the event in their units and distribute the lucky number tickets. Photographic displays of their unit members in action and perhaps recent unit activities would be excellent to have so others can see what members get up to. Then, on the day they can be welcoming, assist with activities, and encourage everyone to take part.

Venue
A place with a large hall, a kitchen, toilets for men and women and plenty of nearby parking.

Age
All ages of girl plus one or two of their nearest relatives. It could be a Rainbow with grandparent, Guide with dad or Brownie with mum, all combinations welcomed.

Guest list
Guests might include prospective Ambassadors, County/Division President, local headteacher. It is important not to have too many people standing around watching, it might put the visiting adults off taking part. Local Commissioners can help with the activities or serve the refreshments: perhaps the visiting times of other guests could be staggered so that they don't all come at once.

Which season?
The advantage of spring or summer time is that with the lighter evening and warmer weather some of the activities could take place out of doors. In contrast, it might be good to have somewhere local and cheap to go during a miserable weekend in October.

Costs involved
- ★ hire of the venue and display boards
- ★ printing of tickets and raffle tickets
- ★ prizes and refreshments
- ★ activity materials

You have to decide whether you're going to make a small charge or ask each unit involved to make a financial contribution.

What to wear
It's helpful if the Guiders and Young Leaders are in uniform but everyone else could be casually dressed.

PR opportunities available
- ★ Send invitations to members of the local community – MPs, youth workers, mayor etc.
- ★ Take photos for distribution after the event with a press release.

Recruitment opportunities to consider
During the event, approach people who are enjoying taking part with a conversation opener for example, 'You seem to be enjoying yourself, were you ever a Guide/Scout?'. However, don't be too pushy, share your enthusiasm, enjoyment and be positive. During refreshments, hand out questionnaires adapted from *The Guide Association Recruitment Toolkit* (see example in Appendices, page 27).

music

 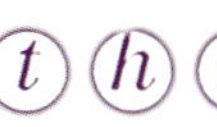   

Aim

An opportunity for all members of the community to be part of a Guiding event within their area. It can be used as a fundraising day and PR opportunity and gives all sections the experience of working together (it is an excellent teambuilding exercise). This can be done on a small or grand scale.

What you need

- ★ first aid cover
- ★ check on copyright for performing rights (see *The Guiding Manual*)
- ★ people to marshal, husbands, partners and fathers etc.
- ★ an organising team
- ★ instruments
- ★ refreshments
- ★ programme
- ★ publicity material
- ★ a security team

Outline of what to do

Music can take many different forms so be as imaginative as you can, this will be the key to a fun event. The outdoor music that is most familiar in Guiding is the campfire songs but there's no reason you couldn't organise a good campfire and invite the local community to join. This will demonstrate that it's not just singing 'ging gang gooli'. Our songs are great and fun, especially with some musical instruments.

Use all the talent you have, a Rainbow unit playing tunes on instruments made in the unit can sound wonderful. A Brownie recorder group, Guide choir, Ranger rock group, Trefoil members learning to play hand chimes. All the girls will have some talent so make the most of it. The more participants the bigger the audience.

If you are working on a large scale event then once you have assembled your team, give each person a specific role. Jobs that need to be undertaken may include co-ordinators for marshalling, refreshments, performers, programme, publicity, organising some security (this is more important if you are making it an open event) etc. You need to decide whether the performers will be from Guiding only, or use local talent or a mixture.

Remember to advise the police that this is going ahead.

Size of event

This will depend on the size of the park or outdoor space available but you can have hundreds present providing that you have enough helpers to marshal the event. Also consider car parking.

Time

Notification

At least six months, but allow more notification if making the show a very large event.

Preparation

Plan well in advance (six months) and consult your local community diary usually held in the library or civic offices so that you do not clash with another youth event. Get a team of interested parties together and brainstorm ideas so that you have booked the performers (if approaching local talent), venue and refreshment area (this will require the use of a marquee).

Venue

A place with outdoor yard (like a school paddock), a large hall, a kitchen, toilets for men and women and plenty of nearby parking will be ideal. If you decided to put the show on in your local park as an 'open' event you will have less control over whom you would like to be present there (which could cause unwelome problems) and you will need to get permission to use the area and to perform.

Age

Everyone can take part and any age group will enjoy coming along.

Guest list

Local civic dignitaries (this will often give extra publicity) and Ambassadors can play a great role in this. Invite Guiding friends from neighbouring Divisions and the County, parents, friends and the general public.

Which season?

June or July when you can hope for some sunshine and hold it in the afternoon (Sundays are preferable).

Costs involved

The venue might be free but some parks or school yards will charge so you may have to negotiate. If you do have to cover this cost (and any others) you could either sell tickets in advance or have a donations box at an entrance stand/table. It is most unlikely that local talent would expect payment as they will see it as a platform for themselves. You could sell refreshments (how about strawberry teas for a summer afternoon?) and cover some expenses this way otherwise, invite people to bring their own picnic.

What to wear

If the girls are the performers then they should be in uniform, unless it is a costumed event. If you are using local talent, then the girls that are helping out with the Guiders should be uniformed.

PR opportunities available

- ★ Invite local press using press release template provided (see Appendices, page 26).
- ★ Distribute flyers and posters to girls and parents at unit meetings, schools, libraries and the local youth groups.
- ★ Approach your local tv and radio station to see if they would like to work with you on the event and perhaps be able to invite acts to attend.

Recruitment opportunities to consider

A wonderful chance to sell Guiding. Your audience should be relaxed at such an event so your recruitment team will have the chance to chat. Make sure you rehearse this part of the day and when best to fit it in. Also, if this is a truly open event, remember that recruitment could focus on girls as well as adults.

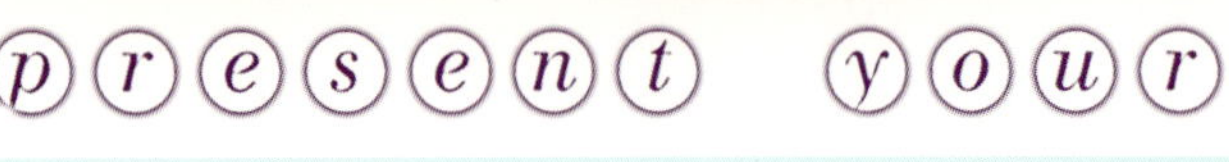

present your own district show

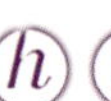

Aim

This is a wonderful opportunity to put Guiding in the 'spotlight'. It will, if 'stage-managed' well, give many people the chance to become involved for a one-off event. Girls from all sections can take part and work together and it gives male helpers a chance to become involved in Guiding. It can be used as a PR exercise, recruitment and fundraising activity.

What you need

★ a lot of enthusiasm from many people
★ some additional time
★ consider any copyright issues (see *The Guiding Manual)*
★ people with skills to perform, or willingness to help eg. musical director, teach circus skills, dance, make costumes, organise lighting, sound etc.

Outline of what to do

Teamwork is the key to success. It is also important to keep everyone informed on progress. Have a get-together with District Guiders, brainstorm what you want in terms of people and material items. Approach anyone outside of Guiding informally (see sample Timetable in the Appendices page 22).

You can produce a medium-scale show as a District using a variety of material eg. a play, musical, circus or another production like a variety show. What you decide to do will probably depend on the talents within the group, so if you had a lot of musicians and singers it might be a good idea to do a musical. The girls love to perform and many have skills so use them! Some girls may not wish to take part but there are other tasks eg. wardrobe, make-up, scenery building, food preparation, front of house etc.

Size of event

This event can be as big as you want it to be but you are advised to start small. However, if you are putting a lot of effort and time into this activity you might want to run the show for at least three performances as this will make the hard work more worthwhile.

Time

Notification

Announce the plans about one year previous, with tickets going on sale two months before the date.

Preparation

Six months.

Accommodation

A large hall or school theatre and a venue for rehearsals.

Age

All sections could take part which would make the performance suitable for a mix of audience.

Guest list

Civic dignitaries, parents, general public, past members of units, Ambassadors.

Which season?

Could be done at any time although to rehearse during the winter months can be good. This enables the show to be ready for spring or summer when the evenings are longer.

Costs involved

All costs should be recovered from the sale of tickets and programme – it might be worth selling tickets in advance so there is some money to work with at the start, or raise the money with a raffle.

What to wear

Performers must have appropriate costume. All others should wear uniform. Helpers not in uniform may feel more a part of the 'team' if they have a special event sweatshirt or t-shirt.

PR opportunities available

★ Invite the general public to come along.
★ Create posters and flyers.
★ Contact your local radio station and invite them to join.
★ If you plan enough in advance, invite a local paper to cover the event from beginning to end, ie. rehearsals, costumes etc. to the actual show.
★ Invite local companies to get involved perhaps by sponsoring a page in the programme.

Recruitment opportunities to consider

Ensure that everyone is aware that recruitment is a very important part of this venture. Use *The Guide Association Recruitment Toolkit* for ideas. Guiders (and Ambassadors) should have a briefing prior to the event to help them prepare and know key points to talk about. A recruitment stand in the entrance and features in the programme are useful tools.

appendices

invitation letter for reception for ambassadors

Put this letter on your County/District headed paper. The central part of your letter could be adapted as a press release. If using it in this way, remember to put 'News Release' at the top and contact details at the end (see the other Template Press Releases on pages 23–26).

<your address
tel. no.
fax no.
email address>

<date>

Dear

Will you be an Ambassador for us?

On behalf of **<number of County members>** members in the County and 700,000 girls and young women in the UK, I would like to invite you to be an Ambassador for The Guide Association.

Ambassadors are special people who recognise the enormous contribution of The Guide Association in offering positive opportunities for girls and young women.

Being an Ambassador is not an onerous task. All we ask is that you say something about Guiding to other people. You don't have to have been in Guiding and you don't have to know about us in detail because we will give you a special Ambassador crib card and a badge of appointment.

On the card you will learn that 50% of the women in this country have been in Guiding at some time, that our leaders are all trained volunteers and that 31% of 8 year old girls are Brownies. You will also see that Guiding in the 21st century is about challenge and fun, about encouraging girls to be the best they can be and to widen their horizons.

The Guide Association is asking all local units, some 34,000, to each find an Ambassador. The Guide County of **<name of your County>** is inviting public figures, business people and local personalities to be its Ambassadors and we are organising a reception at the **<venue>** to celebrate.

We would really like you to be one of our new Ambassadors as your name was suggested as someone who would support the contribution that Guiding makes to the development of girls and young women.

We are looking for a small and exclusive group of people who would be willing to participate in the following ways: **<adapt the following list to fit your needs>**
1) A photocall at the **<venue>** on **<date>** when you will be presented with your badge and card.
2) Agree to wear the badge on suitable occasions and talk to others about Guiding.
3) During each year you are an Ambassador to agree to take part in one local photocall to promote Guiding.

Should you require more information about the role please contact me and I would be delighted to discuss it further.

I do hope that you will feel able to accept this appointment and I look forward to seeing you at the reception.

Yours sincerely,

<your name>
<your role in Guiding>

games for it's a knockout

general notes

- Consider all health and safety issues before the day, not forgetting any allergies. Make sure you have a first aid kit and a trained first aider.
- You need plenty of room for the activities and decorate the 'arena' with colourful bunting, balloons and banners.
- Get yourself a good PA system and play popular, fun music to get everyone in a fun event mood.
- Think about how to organise the games ie. straight relay type games with teams doing same game at the same time, or a 'circus' of games which takes one, two or three teams and everyone moves on to the next game at a given signal.
- Make sure you have enough help to run the games, assist the teams, monitor the PA system and deal with first aid problems.
- Every game could include one team player dressed in a bug costume, to add to the Reach Out and Recruit theme. The bug costume could be shared among players so others get a turn. You'd have to think about different size costumes to fit various age groups.
- It might be a good idea to ask the players to bring a towel and a change of clothes if you're doing the games which involve getting wet.
- For more complicated games to suit Guides, see The Guide Association's Which Game (Trading Service order code: 6369) and adapt any to make challenging for Senior Section members. However, most members will play traditional games no matter what their age.
- If you want to spend money, large inflatables can be hired and there are companies who will organise an 'It's a Knockout' for you.

Blind Bug Slalom

Team
Up to ten players.

Age
All age groups except Rainbows.

Equipment
- 1 blindfold per team
- 1 bug costume
- set of 6 cones or markers per team
- bench to step over or rope with ribbons dangling
- 1 football per team
- 1 bucket per team

How to play
Players stand behind one another with their hands round the waist of the person in front. The first person in each line is dressed as a bug and blindfolded. The rest of the line shout instructions to their bug to steer them round the cones, slalom style, over the bench or rope to the football. The bug must pick up the football, then carry onto the bucket, into which it is dropped, and finally to the end of the course.

How to score
This is a relay type game, first team to finish gains the most points.

Bob and Go

Team
Up to six players.

Age
All age groups.

Equipment
- cardboard boxes with open ends, joined together to make one long tunnel – each team has its own tunnel
- pioneering poles to make simple transporter bridges
- 5 tyres per team
- box of hats
- 1 washing up bowl containing marshmallows sprinkled with flour

How to play
Teams line up at the start point. At the signal, one player heads off through the tunnel, over the bridge, steps in the tyres, goes to the hat box and puts one on, when they reach the marshmallows, they take one with their teeth then dash back to the start. When the first player crosses the start line, the second player can go, and so on until everyone has retrieved a hat and marshmallow.

How to score
First team to finish wins the most points, if you are running it as a circus-type game, time the teams and work out the scores at the end.

games for it's a knockout

Water Bugs

Team
Up to ten people.

Age
All ages.

Equipment
- 2 sets of fins
- 2 snorkels
- 2 rubber rings
- 1 swim hat for each team
- ball pool (can be hired from local inflatable company)
- yellow plastic ducks

How to play
In the ball pool are lots of yellow plastic ducks. Team members take it in turn, from the start line, to dress in the 'water gear' dash to the pool, find a duck and then run back. Second person goes when the first person returns. It's a good idea to have the two sets of 'water gear' available so that the next person can dress while one is running. This game works best as part of a circus of activities.

How to score
Teams are given a set time, say five minutes, to rescue as many ducks as they can. Team with the most ducks wins or the number of ducks can represent the score.

Balloon Bugs

Team
Up to ten players.

Ages
All ages with adaptation.

Equipment
- plenty of balloons partly filled with water
- tall windbreak or screening
- 1 washing up bowl per team

How to play
A bin full of balloons is placed on the start line in front of the team. The course should not be too long. One member of the team goes with the washing up bowl to stand behind the screen. From here, they cannot see the team, and their role is to catch the balloons as they come hurtling over. The rest of the team wait behind the start line. At the signal, the first person picks up a balloon, places it between the knees and moves as quickly as possible to the screen where they toss it over in the hope that the team member will have caught it. If the balloon is dropped or burst during transportation then the player must go back to the start line for another one. Any caught balloons can be recycled, providing the score is kept.

How to score
Teams are given a set time, say five minutes, to get as many balloons as possible over the screen. The team with the greatest number of caught balloons gains the most points.

Bug Jigsaw Relay

Team
Up to six players. The number of jigsaws available will determine how many teams play at a given time.

Age
Especially younger age groups.

Equipment
- large jigsaws pictures of bugs (spiders etc.) made from posters (obtained from zoos or museum) mounted on large pieces of cardboard and then cut into jigsaws of at least eight pieces
- large piece of polythene sheet on which all the jigsaw pieces, except for one piece from each, have been mixed up

How to play
Each team has a different jigsaw and must complete the picture. On the start line, in front of each team, is a piece of jigsaw and at the signal, the first person runs to the pile of jigsaw pieces and picks out a piece to match the one in front of their team. The player then runs back with it and tries to place it in the correct position. Then the second player runs up, finds another piece and so on until the jigsaw is complete.

How to score
First team with complete jigsaw wins the most points. Think about what you will do if someone takes the wrong piece of jigsaw!

it's a knockout

Bug Obstacle Course

Teams
Up to ten people.

Age
All ages except Rainbows.

Equipment
- ★ 10 items of clothing (eg. wig, 2 sets of gloves, scarf, 2 pairs of large wellingtons, shirt, trousers, braces, hat)
- ★ 20 washing up bowls
- ★ a play tunnel (try shops like Argos or the Early Learning Centre)
- ★ 2 hoops with 4 broomsticks with points
- ★ 6 tyres
- ★ scramble net
- ★ 2 large pieces of polythene sheeting
- ★ 2 windbreaks

How to play
The aim is for nine team members to take it in turns to run the course and find pieces of clothing with which they dress the tenth person. One team member at a time goes through the course as follows:
- ★ through the play tunnel
- ★ slides down the 'slippery slope' (ie. a large plastic sheet kept wet and slippy with water and washing up liquid, it helps if there is a slight incline in the obstacle course for the slope)
- ★ through two hoops each of which are staked upright between two broomsticks
- ★ steps in and out of the six tyres
- ★ goes under the scramble net which is positioned over a wet plastic sheet
- ★ reaches the windbreak

Behind the windbreak there are twenty washing up bowls (upside down), under ten of these are items of clothing. If they get a piece of clothing they take it back and put it on their tenth person, if not, they go back empty handed. The game continues until time runs out.

How to score
One point is awarded for every piece of clothing collected and put on the person.

Bug and Spoon Race

Team
Up to six players.

Age
Especially younger age groups.

Equipment
- ★ 4 spoons
- ★ 4 minibugs
- ★ 2 sacks or pieces of thick polythene sheet (big enough for 4 children to stand on) for each team

How to play
This can be done as an egg and spoon race or adapted to include the bug theme. For the bug idea, four children start by standing on one of the pieces of polythene, each with a bug on a spoon and they can only move up the course by standing on polythene stepping stones. At the signal, the other two players bring the second piece of polythene round in front of them. The foursome then transfer themselves with bugs on spoons onto this while the pair fetch the first piece of polythene to put in front of them. The game continues in this way until they reach the end of the course.

How to score
The first team to the end wins the most points.

Wet Bugs

Team
Two teams are needed, team A, (the defenders) consist of two people. Team B are the players, with six people.

Age
All ages.

Equipment
- ★ paddling pool filled with water
- ★ loads of balls
- ★ 2 dustbins

How to play
The paddling pool is positioned within reasonable throwing distance of the dustbins which contain the balls. The balls shouldn't be too heavy or hard in case they hit one of the players. The distance from the bins to the paddling pool depends upon the age and ability of the players. The two players from team A must throw out any balls that land in the pool and they should be suitably dressed to stand in the pool and get wet. Four players from team B attempt to throw balls from the marker by the bin into the pool. The other two team B players have the task of collecting the balls thrown out of the pool and putting them into the dustbins for their team mates.

How to score
Team B is given a fixed amount of time, say five minutes, in which to get balls into the pool. When the time's up, team A players must stop throwing balls from the pool. Those that remain in the pool are counted up. At the end of the game, the team that had the most balls in the pool wins.

timetable for your district show

September

- ★ Hold a meeting with participants (this can include older Guides or Senior Section) to find out what skills are available and decide on the production.
- ★ Collect together the music (a music library is a good starting place).
- ★ Meet with the musical director.
- ★ Think of a way to raise some funds and book the venue for the show and rehearsals.

October

- ★ Send a letter to members inviting them to take part (as performers or helpers).
- ★ Write letters to parents asking permission for their daughters to take part, invite parents to become involved by offering specific jobs.
- ★ Organise a get together with those interested in taking part to find out what skills are available.
- ★ Production team meeting to discuss how and when you will rehearse.

November

- ★ Hold an informal evening for all the people responsible for different areas of your show. Nominate a team leader for each of the following where applicable: wardrobe, lighting, sound, scenery, make-up, dance, music, business, PR, recruitment, front of house, tickets, other helpers.

December

- ★ Production team meeting with key people, ie. director, stage manager, musical director, wardrobe, make-up, front of house etc.

January to March

- ★ Rehearsals, costumes made, props and set prepared, lighting and sound organised.

April

- ★ Dress rehearsals and technical rehearsal.

Easter

- ★ Performance.

template press release

This is a template, please feel free to modify it to meet the needs of your event.

News Release

Guides Make Mothering Sunday Special

<date>
<for immediate release>
<press release number>

Local **<Rainbows, Brownies, Guides, Senior Section>**, made Mothers Day that extra bit special at a party held in honour of their hardworking mums.

On **<date>** members got together to show their mums just what they get up to in **<Rainbows/Brownies/Guides/Senior Section>**, and also to let them join in on some of the fun they have every week at meetings.

The girls treated their mums to a variety of activities such as **<facials, crafts, music, comedy>**, and ended the evening serving their guests with **<dinner/sandwiches/tea>**.

As **<leader/District Commissioner>** said:

'Everyone involved in the event had a great time. The girls were given the chance to show off some of their skills and see what girls gain from Guiding in **<local area>**.' The mums were given the opportunity to relax and be pampered for their special day.

ENDS

For further information please contact **<your name and contact details>**.

Notes to Editor

- ★ The Guide Association is the UK's largest voluntary youth organisation for girls and young women.
- ★ **<number>** of members attended the Mothers Day event in **<area>**.
- ★ There are **<number>** of Guide Association members in **<your area>**.
- ★ To find out more about Guiding in **<your area>**, call **<your number>** or 0800 1 69 59 01.

template

press release

This is a template, please feel free to modify it to meet the needs of your event.

If you are organising the Fashion Show as a closed event, ie. with parents and family only, then release this after the occasion with a photo. If it's an open invitation then make sure you give clear details on tickets and where they are available.

News Release

Guides Hit the Catwalk

<date>
<for immediate release>
<press release number>

Forget London, Paris or Milan, there is a fashion show happening much nearer than you think! Local **<Brownies/Guides>** are holding their very own fashion show, that will give them the chance to show off their hidden talents and fashion sense!

Not wanting to be the same as every other model in town, the girls from **<your area>**, will be holding a show with a difference. Instead of modelling the latest fashions, the **<Brownies/Guides>** will be doing an alternative show, entitled **<theme of the fashion show>**.

Guests will be able to see the girls imaginations run wild as they show off their catwalk styles.

There will also be time afterwards to enjoy refreshments laid on by the **<Brownies/Guides>**.

The Guide Association in **<your area>** allows girls and young women the chance to experience many fun activities. Every week members have the opportunity to participate in **<examples of what you do>**.

Tickets for this event are limited so don't delay! **<give details of tickets and how to obtain them>**

ENDS

For further information and photographs contact **<your name and contact details>**

Notes to Editor

- ★ The Guide Association is the UK's largest voluntary youth organisation for girls and young women.
- ★ **<number>** members attended the Fashion Show in **<area>**.
- ★ There are **<number>** Guide Association members in **<your area>**.
- ★ To find out more about Guiding in **<your area>**, call **<your number>** or 0800 1 69 59 01.

This is a template, please feel free to modify it to meet the needs of your event.

News Release

A Feast of Family Fun

<date>
<for immediate release>
<press release number>

There was laughter in the air on **<date>** when **<Rainbows/Brownies/Guides/Senior Section>** from **<your area>** all met in **<venue>** for a Family Fun Day.

The event, organised by the local **<District/Division>** brought together family members to experience the enjoyment and skills that young people, and the adults working with them, gain from being a part of the Association.

Everyone took part in a wide range of activities such as **<list activities, ie. face painting, stalls, etc>**, and had the opportunity to see what Guiding has to offer people.

As **<leader/District Commissioner>** comments:

'The day was a great success, and gave members of The Guide Association a chance to show families what they get up to in **<Rainbow/Brownie/Guide>** meetings. They experienced first-hand the fun that all our members have, and went away having learnt a lot more about Guiding in **<local area>**. We also gained some more recruits as helpers and members.'

ENDS

For further information please contact **<your name and contact details>**.

Notes to Editor

- ★ The Guide Association is the UK's largest voluntary youth organisation for girls and young women.
- ★ **<number>** of members attended the Family Fun Day in **<area>**.
- ★ There are **<number>** of Guide Association members in **<your area>**.
- ★ To find out more about Guiding in **<your area>**, call **<your number>** or 0800 1 69 59 01 .

This is a template, please feel free to modify it to meet the needs of your event.

News Release

Let's Get Musical!

<date>
<for immediate release>
<press release number>

On **<date>**, **<Rainbows, Brownies and Guides>** in **<local area>** are joining **<number of people>** at a special concert in **<location>**.

On this day, **<musicians from Guiding/all around the area or showcase for new talent>** will have a chance to join in and entertain the audience.

There will be **<details of your event>**.

Families are welcome to come along, listen to the music and find out what The Guide Association and its members are getting up to in its area.

As **<local volunteer>** said:

'This event will be a great opportunity for the local community to get together and see what girls can do in The Guide Association. Long gone are the days of just singing campfire songs – there is a lot of musical talent and festival skills in the girls in our unit. Who knows, we could be seeing the new Popstars or Vanessa Mae on stage!'

ENDS

For further information about attending the event, or to arrange a photocall or interview with a local member of The Guide Association, please contact **<your name and contact details>**.

Notes to Editor

- ★ The Guide Association is the UK's largest voluntary youth organisation for girls and young women.
- ★ There will be **<number of attendees>** visiting **<name of your event>**.
- ★ Local VIPs such as **<MP/Mayor/celebrity>** will be attending.
- ★ There will be **<special event>** happening at **<time and area>**.

questionnaire

***This is a sample questionnaire that you could use with event attendees. Feel free to modify it to your specific event or needs. You will also find more examples in* The Guide Association Recruitment Toolkit.**

Dear Guest

We hope you have enjoyed yourself at our **<fun event>**. To help us think about future activities it would be really helpful if you could complete this form. One of our Guiders will collect it from you.

Thank you
<name of Guider in charge>

1. Have you had an enjoyable time?

---

2. What have you enjoyed most about the day/event?

---

3. Were you ever a Brownie ☐ Guide ☐ Ranger ☐ Leader ☐ or in Scouts ☐? (tick as appropriate)

4.What was the best thing about being in Guiding for you?

---

5. What does your daughter/stepdaughter/granddaughter/ward enjoy most about Guiding?

---

6. If we were to offer another event similar to this **<or such as x>** would you be prepared to:

☐ help on the day ☐ help with the advance planning
☐ offer to run the event

Depending on the new event, other tasks might include
☐ sell tickets ☐ help out backstage
☐ prepare the programme ☐ co-ordinate an element of the event

7. In our unit/District/Division we have identified that if we had **<1–3>** adults/women volunteers, of whom one could come to each meeting, we would be able to **<these are just examples>**

☐ take six girls off the waiting list ☐ give regular leaders occasional nights off
☐ be able to offer the girls a more adventurous programme

Would you consider helping one week in three? (about three times a term)
☐ I don't know, but tell me more ☐ Possibly, what would I have to do?
☐ No, I can't come that often but I could offer to help at a special meeting to teach a skill
☐ I can't attend meetings, are there other ways I could help
☐ Other

Thanks very much
P.S. Did you know 50% of women in the UK have been members at some point in their lives? We have 70,000 trained adult volunteer leaders; we have 30,000 volunteer helpers and support people. Most of our leaders and helpers work, have homes and families.

evaluation form

The team that put this booklet together would appreciate your feedback on the ideas it contains. Please return the form (or a photocopy is fine) to Membership Development Team, The Guide Association, 17–19 Buckingham Palace Road, London, SW1W 0PT or fax it on 020 7630 6199.

Thank you
Reach Out and Recruit Working Group 2001

Which event(s) have you tried?

Did members and guests have an enjoyable time?

What image or message about Guiding do you think the event gave?

How did you use the event for PR or Recruitment?

What were the outcomes of the event?

What did you learn for the future?

Would you do another event from the booklet for PR or Recruitment?

Why?

What more help would you like with PR or Recruitment?

Have you seen/used/incorporated ideas from *The Guide Association Recruitment Toolkit*?

Do you have any other ideas that could be used for a future publication on recruitment?